ADAM L.S.

# The Forest

*First published by Raguel Studios 2024*



*First edition*

*Illustration by Karen Keeline*

*This book was professionally typeset on Reedsy.*
*Find out more at reedsy.com*

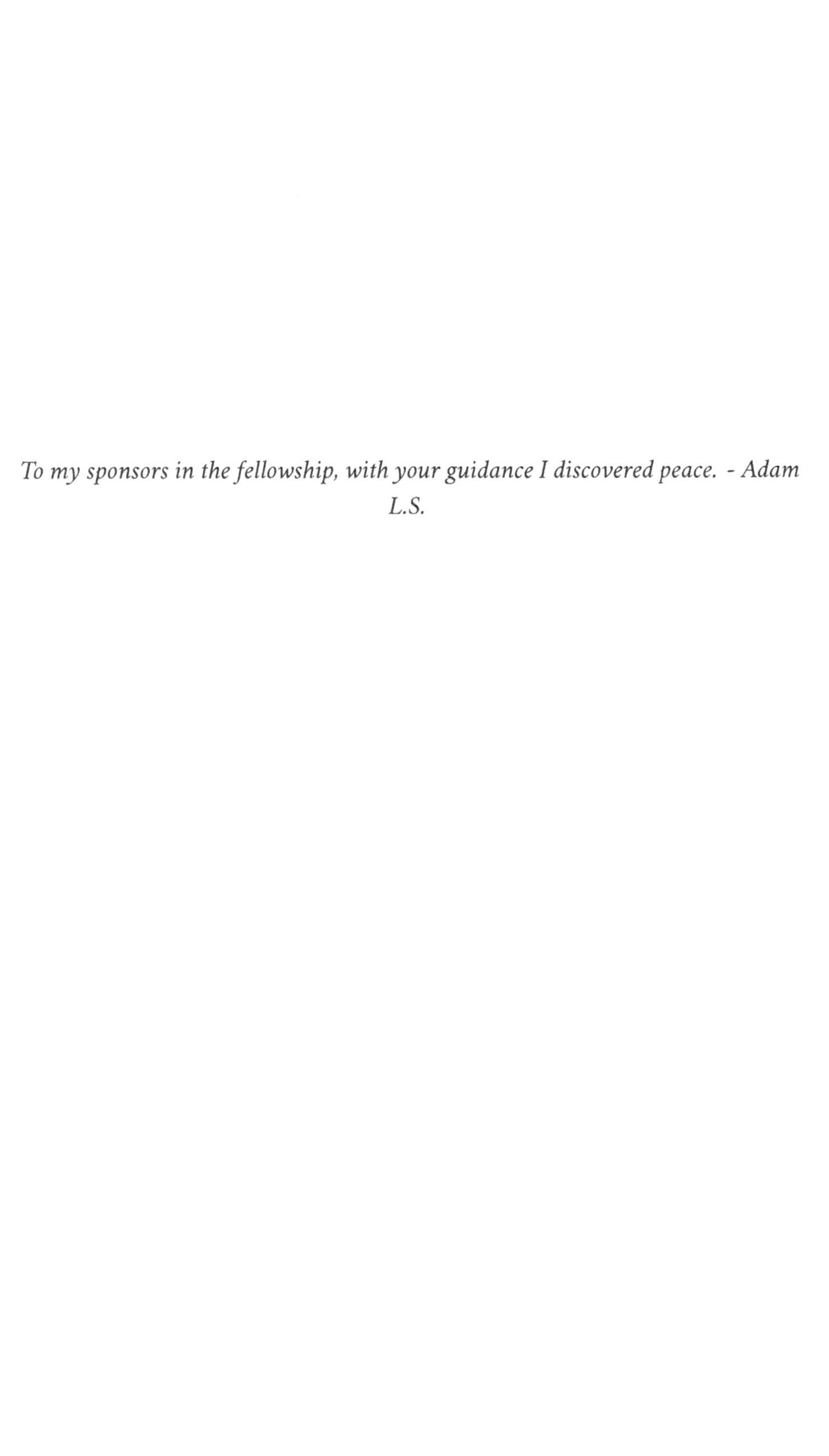

*To my sponsors in the fellowship, with your guidance I discovered peace. - Adam L.S.*

Right now. - Adam L.S.

# Contents

# Acknowledgments

To those of you recommending books to me, I've enjoyed them so much. - Adam L.S.

# I

# Chapter 1: Breathe

# Universe

Who am I?
  Enabled, important…

What do I do?
  Allow your story to unfold…

Adam. L.S.

# Welcome

Rise above thought,
   free the mind.
   Enlightenment.

The truth is located within.

My origin, my body's reaction,
   my body became weightless.
   Emotion.

Adam. L.S.

# The Way Out

No more pain?
  Dissolve it.

No more ego?
  Identify the pain and fear.

I became conscious, I became whole.

Adam. L.S.

# Movers

I moved to the present.
  Away from the delusion of time.

I found a key to a new dimension.

Adam. L.S.

# Momentum

Urgently, I sought transformation,
 of human consciousness.

I desired momentum,
 I wanted to live and be present.

The effect was life changing.

Adam. L.S.

# Somebody Else

The spiritual teacher is here...
  Outlining anxiety, depression, the past...

It all felt like somebody else,
  once I learned to live in the present.

Adam. L.S.

# Probably

I awoke feeling absolute dread,
  that same silent dream was more intense than it had ever been.

Was it utterly meaningless?

Probably not,
  I carried a burden of misery,
  I felt a deep loathing of the world,
  I struggled to exist,
  I longed for my own annihilation.

Adam. L.S.

# Stronger

I became much stronger,
  I finally had a desire to live.

I kept repeating this in my mind.
  I became self aware.

Adam. L.S.

# Vortex

This strange realization,
   I was fully conscious, fully aware.

I was gripped,
   by a vortex of energy.

I started to shake,
   I stopped resisting.

Adam. L.S.

# Dawn

My eyes had been closed,
  Not yet fully awakened.

When they opened,
  I saw the light of dawn.

Infinitely more than I ever imagined,
  pure love, tears filled my eyes.

So alive,
  so much beauty.

Adam. L.S.

# Amazed

I am utterly amazed at the miracle of life,
  born into this beautiful world.

Obtaining a state of uninterrupted deep peace and bliss.
  It became my natural state.

Adam. L.S.

# Toy

That intense pressure of suffering,
  forced my consciousness to withdraw.

My unhappy, fear drenched self,
  was maybe fiction?

I let the air out of that inflatable toy.

Adam. L.S.

# Benched

There formed…
  A timeless, deathless realm.

Left with nothing…
  I sat on a park bench, feeling intense joy.

Adam. L.S.

# Teacher.

I had it, but could not feel it.
  My mind made too much noise.

The time came, I held it in my hand,
  spirituality, I wish I could teach this subject.

Adam. L.S.

# Truth Serum

Is the truth inside us?
  Do we all seek a deeper love and appreciation?

I had to embrace change.
  I had to embrace that truth.

Adam. L.S.

# Worthy

I wanted to be worthy,
  worthy of a full life.

I wanted that seed of life to sprout.
  I learned to meditate.

Adam. L.S.

# False

Everything I felt was false,
  it drew my attention constantly.

Dysfunctional, behavioral manifestations,
  creating warfare among any tribe I encountered.

I learned to recognize false for false,
  as a man I did not want to associate with.

I sought a lasting transformation,
  I no longer was drawn into the illusion,
  I no longer formed pain.

Adam. L.S.

# Everyday

I wanted another level…
  I wanted to let go of my personal problems,
  I wanted all those bright future possibilities.

They are available,
  they just require me to be free.

That level,
  that enlightened state.

Adam. L.S.

# Seed

Designed for concern,
  again and again.

Timeless, intense conscious presence,
  in the now, thru this passage, a rewarding taste.

That seed of enlightenment.

Adam. L.S.

# Reach

Think, think, think…
  How do I reach that deeper self,
  deeper truth,
  deeper meaning?

It resonates strength!
  I began studying.
  I wanted to live there forever.

Adam. L.S.

# Keep Going

Read on,
  clear away the irrelevant.

Read on,
  into yourself.

Adam. L.S.

# Remember

I had to watch out for responding so quickly,
I had to be reminded, I could not forget.

I had to remember how it felt,
in every cell, every muscle in my body.

Nothing compared to that feeling,
that confusion.

So I sought other teachings,
teachings of happiness.

Adam. L.S.

# Left Alone

Conscious now, of the stepping stones,
  their trans-formative power.

I never wanted to feel lost,
  or left alone again.

Adam. L.S.

# Right Here

Followers and teachers,
  no need to go elsewhere for the truth.

It's right here.
  Inside.

Adam. L.S.

# Yes

That timeless, spiritual lesson,
  heightened aliveness...

Yes, I know, this is true.

Adam. L.S.

# Box

My greatest obstacle to this...
  Enlightened state?

I sat by the side of the road,
  strangers passing by,
  with nothing in my pocket,
  a box, discovered...
  I wondered, what's inside?
  Ever looked in? Nope...
  Pry it open!

It was filled, but not with gold...
  with heart.

Adam. L.S.

# Listen

I am. I am not.
   I exist.

I hear you.

Adam. L.S.

# Rich

I found true wealth.
  I radiated joy.

Fulfillment, validation, security, love,
  I'm so wealthy, now.

Adam. L.S.

# Things

All those things,
greater than anything the world could offer.

Are within.

Adam. L.S.

# Accomplished

I felt, accomplished!
  Ego scared it away, for so long.

Oneness, connectedness,
  immeasurable, indestructible?

Paradoxically essential,
  beyond name and form.

I rid myself of ego,
  and the illusion of feeling separated from the world.

Adam. L.S.

# Maybe

This life, that life, the next...

Precaution?
  Nah.

Enlightenment?
  Maybe.

Adam. L.S.

# Just That

Please explain,
  what you meant by that.

One life?
  Ever present?
  Eternal?
  Birth, and death?
  A myriad of forms?
  An indestructible essence?

Adam. L.S.

# Now

What was my true nature?
  Then? Now? Tomorrow?
  Be still!

Just…
  Now.

Adam. L.S.

# Sacred

The meaning of the word God...
  Misused?

Use it...
  Sparingly?

I caught a glimpse,
  of the realm of the sacred.

It's vastness,
  infinite.

Adam. L.S.

# Part

Those absurd beliefs,
  assumptions, assertions, delusions.

Part of it.

Adam. L.S.

# Being

Was I helping or hindering?
  Just being, a being.

What a concept.
  Being an infinite entity.

Adam. L.S.

# Stop It?

The obstacle to reality is...
  To identify yourself?
  Your mind?

To stop...
  Thinking.

Adam. L.S.

# Mind Made

The noise in my head was incessant,
  I could not be still.

This mind made self had to go,
  it's shadow was dreadful.

Adam. L.S.

# What?

I think, therefore I am?
  Fundamental truths?
  Identify with thinking?!

This world is insanely complex!

Adam. L.S.

# The Beginning

The end…
  Of suffering.
  Conflict within, and without.
  Incessant, and dreadful thinking.

This is…
  Incredible.
  May be liberation.
  Is said to be enlightenment.

Adam. L.S.

# Comforted

Once I felt oneness,
  I felt comforted,
  comforted by...

The present.

I was no longer plagued by thoughts of
  the past, present, or future.

Adam L.S.

# Existence

I was possessed.
  Possessed by thought.

I observed the entity,
  the thinker.

Something activated,
  I traveled beyond thought,
  to a vast realm.
Where I found consciousness.
  There, I could see all things that truly matter.

Adam L.S.

# Voices

I told you, I hear voices.
   Wait, so do you?
   Yes, several.

Mad ones,
   happy ones.

They are irrelevant.

Adam L.S.

# Movies

These movies, in my mind,
  won't stop.

They revive the past,
  rehearse a future.

I loved the movies, however,
  I had to stop watching them...

To be free.

Adam L.S.

# It Is Me

I realize, the voice is real,
   and here I am, listening to it, observing it.

It is me, it is my presence,
   coming alive from beyond my mind.

Adam L.S.

# I Had To

I had to…
Listen to thought,
Be aware of thought,
Witness thought.

I found a new dimension.
I had to find out.

Adam. L.S.

# Energizer

Recalling those moments,
  energized my mind.

I decided,
  my thoughts would no longer be involuntary.

Adam. L.S.

# Sup

The joy from just being.
  Being alive
  Being present.

Adam. L.S.

# Flow

Every time I'd walk up,
  Every movement,
  Every breath…

Thru it all,
  I was present.
  I observed the flow.
  I found peace within.

Adam. L.S.

# Wow

Your hands,
  The way you close the door…

Your scent,
  The way your head bobbled…

Wow.

Adam. L.S.

# Journey

I had to go,
  on that journey I stumbled across something.

I heard a voice,
  I caught myself smiling.

Adam. L.S.

# Leaks

Most of my thinking was repetitive,
  maybe useless?

At times it felt dysfunctional,
  maybe negative?

There was a serious leakage of vital energy.

Adam. L.S.

# Win

I was addicted to thinking,
   overly compulsive.

It gave me a sense of pleasure,
   however it would always turn to pain.

It would not be stronger than me,
   so I made a choice, I stopped.

Adam. L.S.

# Sense of Self

I was scared,
  that I'd cease to be,
  if my mind was not active.

Would my sense of self be lost?

Adam. L.S.

# Observe

To be ok…
  to be at peace…
  to be in the present…

I could see, but I would misperceive.
  I'd look through eyes of the past.
  It would reduce the present, always lying.

To be ok…
  I observed how my mind worked.

Adam. L.S.

# Moment

Keys jangled.
  But I was still locked out.

I wanted to be free.
  I wanted to be in each moment.

I am…
  My mind.

Adam. L.S.

# Gift

I had to analyze,
I had to learn,
I had to be clear.
I had to be more focused.
I received the gift of thought.
I don't want to lose my mind.
I don't want to be another species of animal.

Adam. L.S.

# He Can Not Exist

The monster attacked my mind,
  it was urgent that I destroy him.

At this stage,
  I evolved.

Adam. L.S.

# Parts

I knew I'd fall down,
  it's part of life.

I refused to fall backward,
  I rose above those thoughts.

I focused,
  I found a way.

I felt free,
  I felt inner stillness.

Adam. L.S.

# I Really Do

I'd oscillate,
  between thought and stillness.

I like to be creative,
  I like finding solutions.

We seem connected,
  don't you think?

Adam. L.S.

# Shhhhh!

My mind is a survival machine!
  Isn't yours as well?

Gathering, storing, analyzing,
  so much information.

Lets try some mental quietude,
  for now.

Adam. L.S.

# Power On

I kept learning how it all worked,
my mind and body.

Read, stretch, breathe, speak, race.

It's all connected,
I just need to reconnect with it.

Adam. L.S.

# Engineer

These tools are absolutely wonderful,
greater than I ever could have imagined.

Mind.
Body.

Adam. L.S.

# Rocket

My emotions would rise,
  like a sky rocket.

I'd react,
  that was my pattern.

To every hostile thought,
  or action.

It was all a reflection,
  of my mind and body.

Adam. L.S.

# Bio

I built up so much energy,
  so much anger.

Always ready for a fight,
  feeling threatened, for some reason.

My body would contract,
  out of fear.

My biochemistry was so messed up.

Adam. L.S.

# Energy Field

I began focusing my attention on my inner energy field.
I could feel my body from within.

Adam. L.S.

# Conflicted

My mind said no way!
  My emotions said yes!

Or the other way around.

Adam. L.S.

# Hmmm...

Is anybody entirely free of pain and sorrow?
  How do I find the way out?
  Could I learn to live with them?
  Rather than avoid them?

Adam. L.S.

# The Show

This is so unnecessary,
  all of this pain.

Wait. I'm learning,
  something.

Wait. Just listen,
  observe.

It will not run my life.

Adam. L.S.

# Bemused

What time is it?
  What day is it?
  Does it matter?

The orchid and the crow would be bemused.

It's now.
  What else is there?

Adam. L.S.

# Direction

I began to observe,
  watching my own presence.

There was a light,
  a light of consciousness.

So I asked myself,
  what is going on inside me at this moment?

I believe,
  I'm heading in the right direction.

Adam. L.S.

# Doorway

There was an energy,
  I could feel it…

As I passed thru that doorway.

Adam. L.S.

# Residual

There was a residual,
  pain from my past.

Accumulating so much of it,
  made me dizzy.

I no longer wanted any of it,
  I decided to be done creating pain for myself and for others.

Adam. L.S.

# Heard

Yes!

You heard me.

Yes!

I want something different.
Ok… I'll try living in the present.

Adam. L.S.

# Resisting

Stop resisting, they said.
  I did not believe I was.

But I was.
  That was part of my pattern.

I was, unhappy.

Adam. L.S.

# Friendship

I was terrified of life.
 Until we became friends.

It was a miraculous transformation.

Adam. L.S.

# It's Beautiful Here, Now

It was lodged in there,
 all that pain.

I was emotional,
 it just lived on inside of me.

I suffered as a child,
 and for so many years after.

I was unconscious of the world that I was born into.

Adam. L.S.

# Watch Out

I loved to engage,
  in reckless, dangerous behavior.

Without insurance.
  never assured of whom I really was.

Stage 4.

Adam. L.S.

# Turn Signal

This may mean death,
  we met, spoke for a bit.

Not yet, death.
  I'm heading back.

I chose life.

Adam. L.S.

# Dang.

It was a life threatening emergency,
  living in that dimension.

So I chose this one,
  where I write, and smile.

Adam. L.S.

# Tree

I looked out the window...

The colors of that tree outside,
 seemed brighter, more vibrant.

There was something invisible, its essence.
 I hadn't truly seen the tree before.

We are connected.

# Weightless

All this time...
How could I use this time?

I had to maneuver,
thru psychological time,
or I'd be stuck in the time warp, again.

Future projections are not as important,
as whats right in front of me.

My watch broke,
I no longer leap thru time.

Adam. L.S.

# Law

The law of time,
  predictions,
  lessons.

These patterns...
  We keep learning...
  We keep going.

Adam. L.S.

# Transformer

I wish I could transform,
  time, me.

Totally aware of time now,
  of the past,
  I learned a lot.

I am free of psychological time now.

Adam. L.S.

# Forgiven

Dwelling on guilt,
  mistakes, me, mine.

It was heavy,
  all that burden.

I let go of the false sense of identity I had created,
  non forgiveness is not a requirement for living.

I finally forgave.

Adam. L.S.

# Honor

I gave them my full attention attention,
   each breathe, each step.

I now honor it,
   this path, the present, everything, everyone.

Adam. L.S.

# Going Without

Without that mental disease,
  insanity, those ideologies and manifestations.

I'm finally who I was meant to be.
  The best version of me.

Adam. L.S.

# Dirt

The roots were covered in negativity and suffering,
the bark seemed dreadful, and the leaves, even the buds wilted.

I dissolved the past,
replaced the soil.

That's when I began shaping a healthier future.

Adam. L.S.

# Happy, Happy, Happy

I believed, happiness did not exist.

The fact is…
  I can be free now.

And it does.

Adam. L.S.

# Hope

That piece the wall read…
  Hope.

It existed there.
  It still exists somewhere, I'm sure.

It's here, now and it keeps me going.

Adam. L.S.

# What's This?

Full of it...
  Problems.

No room for it...
  Solutions.

What's this...
  Space?

It's...
  Life!

Adam. L.S.

# The Forest

This space allows everything to be,
  in it, there's silence, under the sounds.

I feel the wind, flowing in and out.

I moved deep into the forest,
  there I found the life energy.

Adam. L.S.

# Paradise

All my problems were illusions,
  I temporarily evaded matters and emotions.

The fact of the matter is that there were no problems,
  I did not need to take time to survive.

Realizing this, I found paradise,
  in the present.

Adam. L.S.

# Evolving

There was a quantum leap in my evolution,
  they were no longer just glimpses of freedom.

This change was inevitable,
  for my survival.

Adam. L.S.

# Both

No matter what I was doing I asked myself,
  do I feel happy, do I feel joyful?

When I was present, I was both.
  Time could no longer cover that up.

Adam. L.S.

# Loved

I loved problems,
  They provided me some identity.

Even when overwhelmed,
  by the burden of 100 things.

Life is challenging enough,
  and I added a bit of pain on to each moment.

I became fed up with it all,
  I no longer wanted to contaminate this beautiful world.

Adam. L.S.

# Had To

I had to…
   continue, to pursue my goals.

The future would not save me,
   or make me happy.

I had to…
   let go, of these illusory expectations.

I was already complete.

Adam L.S.

# Real

A playful, joyus energy exists,
  behind the things we do...

So I was told.

I was so caught up in permanency,
  I was so entangled with fear.

This is a world of birth,
  there is an eternal underneath,
  and nothing real can be threatened.

Adam L.S.

# Wake Up!

I felt like I was in a constant dream state,
   a dreamless sleep at that, just wandering around.

Unease, boredom and nervousness,
   were the highlights.

I began showing up,
   for activities.

They brought me a sense of joy,
   so I woke up.

Adam L.S.

# Do You Get It?

With all these tense conversations,
  stares, and this cruel demeanor…

What was I seeking, wanting or craving?

Adam L.S.

# Also by Adam L.S.

The Class is poetry exploring economies, families, relationships; what it takes to determine the climate of each and reconstruct each as needed, if needed, to build a stronger bond.

**The Class**
Coming soon!

www.ingramcontent.com/pod-product-compliance
Lightning Source LLC
LaVergne TN
LVHW050316160826
845677LV00014B/3428

*9798230861485*